INDIGENOUS AMERICAN CULTURES

Celebrating the CHEROKEE

ANNE ACCARDI

Mitchell Lane
PUBLISHERS

Parent and Caregiver Tips for Creating Nonfiction Readers

The high-interest topics in the ***Indigenous American Cultures*** series are sure to get your young reader excited about reading nonfiction. While exploring a fascinating subject, your reader will be introduced to new facts, ideas, and vocabulary.

Tips for Reading Nonfiction

Talk about Nonfiction

Explain that nonfiction books provide facts about real-world topics. When readers read nonfiction, they gain a rich understanding of the world. They build background knowledge that provides a foundation for learning and academic success.

Look at the Parts

This book contains the following helpful features. Share the purpose of each feature with your reader.

Photos, Captions, and Graphic Aids
The photos, captions, maps, diagrams, time lines, and other graphic aids in nonfiction texts contain a wealth of information. Help your reader identify different ways information can be displayed.

Sidebars
These extra tidbits of information help satisfy readers' curiosity and expand their knowledge.

Table of Contents
Located at the front of the book, this list shows the big ideas within the text and the page numbers where they can be found.

Glossary
Located at the back of the book, the glossary defines key words and phrases that are related to the topic. These words and phrases can be found in the text in colored type.

Comprehension Questions (Fact Check)
Multiple-choice questions help readers self-check to make sure they understand what they read.

Index
Located at the back of the book, the index is an alphabetical list of topics and the page numbers where they can be found.

With a little help and guidance, your reader will be on their way to enjoying and learning from nonfiction books.

Mitchell Lane
PUBLISHERS
mitchelllanepub.com

2001 SW 31st Avenue
Hallandale, FL 33009

First Edition, 2026.
Author: Anne Accardi
Designer: Rhea Magaro
Editor: Kim Thompson

Series: Indigenous American Cultures
Title: Celebrating the Cherokee / by Anne Accardi

Hallandale, FL : Mitchell Lane Publishers, [2026]

Library bound ISBN: 979-8-89260-551-9
Paperback ISBN: 979-8-89260-587-8
eBook ISBN: 979-8-89260-562-5

PHOTO CREDITS
Alamy: Buddy Mays, cover, 1, 26; FLHC DBJU3, 6; North Wind Picture Archives, 7; Shelley Dennis, 9; Danvis Collection, 12; Cinematic, 17; NB/TRAN, 20; Pictorial Press Ltd, 27; Danita Delimont, 28; Public Domain: 5; Dave Berry Photography, 21; Library of Congress, 13; Wiki, 5, 10, 15; Shutterstock: SketchMonsterFamily, cover, all; gomolach, cover, 1, 3, 4, 6, 10, 14, 16, 22, 26, 28; Donna Bollenbach, cover, 1, 5; Uswatun des, cover, 1, 18; RaksyBH, cover, 1, 13; RodClementPhotography, 9; JNix, 11; sdx15, 14; Ted PAGEL, 16; eurobanks, 18; LinnB, 18; Paul Pellegrino, 18; Sergio Hayashi, 19; Janny2, 21; Silver Spiral Arts, 21; Vineyard Perspective, 22, 24, 25; Kim Kelley-Wagner, 23; s_bukley, 26; MarkVanDykePhotography, 29

CONTENTS

A Cherokee Connection 4
Cherokee History 6
Exploring Cherokee Places 10
The Cherokee Language 14
Honoring Cherokee Traditions 16
Cherokee Celebrations 22
Famous Faces 26
Lessons from the Cherokee 28
Glossary 30
Fact Check 31
Further Reading 31
On the Internet 31
Index 32
About the Author 32

A CHEROKEE CONNECTION

While driving through the southeastern United States, you might see signs for the Unicoi Turnpike Trail. This 150-mile (240-kilometer) trail is one of the oldest paths in North America. It has been used for thousands of years.

Long ago, the trail connected the Cherokee city of Chota to towns near the Atlantic Ocean. People used it to trade goods and move fighters during battles. The trail is a reminder that Cherokee people have lived on this continent for **eons**. They continue to influence America in important ways.

Culture Close-Up

The Unicoi Turnpike Trail runs through the Cherokee National Forest. This vast forest extends to the Great Smoky Mountains, an area that is **sacred** to the Cherokee people.

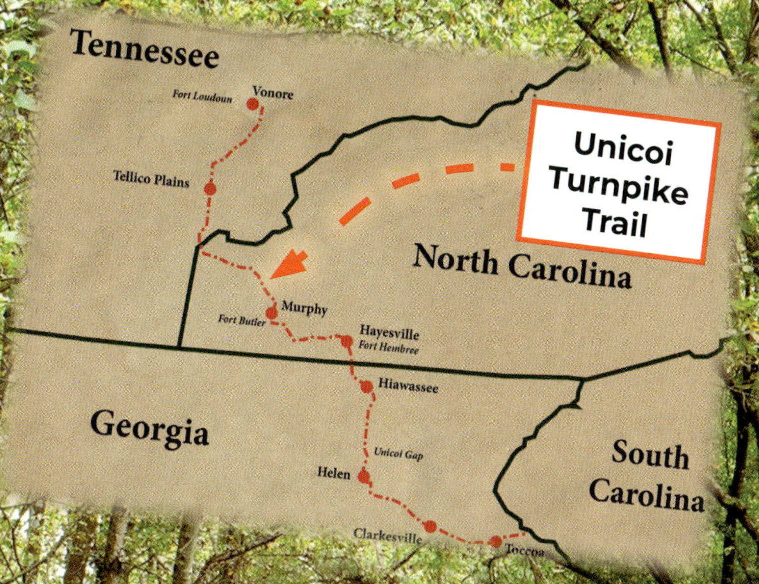
Tennessee
Fort Loudoun
Vonore
Tellico Plains
Unicoi Turnpike Trail
North Carolina
Murphy
Fort Butler
Hayesville
Fort Hembree
Hiawassee
Georgia
Unicoi Gap
Helen
Clarkesville
Toccoa
South Carolina

GEORGIA
1776
THE UNICOI TURNPIKE
This road is the Old Unicoi Turnpike, first vehicular route to link East Tennessee, Western North Carolina and North Georgia with the head of navigation on the Savannah River system. Beginning on the Tugalo River, to the east of Toccoa, the road led this way, thence through Unicoi Gap and via Murphy, N.C. to Nine Mile Creek near Maryville, Tenn.
Permission to open the way as a toll road was given by the Cherokees in 1813 to a Company of Indians and white men. Tennessee and Georgia granted charters to the concern.
Prior to its establishment as a road, the trace was part of a trading path from Augusta to the Cherokees in East Tennessee.
154-1R
GEORGIA HISTORICAL MARKER

CHEROKEE HISTORY

Over 400 years ago, Cherokees lived throughout the Appalachian Mountains. They had a complex network of towns and villages. They farmed, used tools, made baskets and **pottery**, and voted on laws for their people. Cherokee homelands are now parts of West Virginia, Kentucky, Virginia, North Carolina, Tennessee, South Carolina, Georgia, and Alabama.

Europeans arrived in the 1600s. The Cherokee began trading clothes, metal, and weapons with the **colonizers**.

In 1828, American **settlers** found gold on Cherokee land and wanted it. President Andrew Jackson helped pass a law that ordered the Cherokee to leave their homes. Cherokee Principal Chief John Ross tried to convince the United States government to let his people stay. But soldiers forced thousands to move west on a difficult and deadly journey. The terrible trip came to be called the Trail of Tears. It ended in present-day Oklahoma.

Today, Cherokees are one of the largest tribal groups in the U.S. They include the Cherokee Nation, the Eastern Band of Cherokee Indians, and the United Keetoowah Band of Cherokee Indians.

More than 140,000 people live on the Cherokee Nation **reservation** in northeast Oklahoma.

Culture Close-Up

The oldest surviving government building in Oklahoma is a Cherokee courthouse built in 1844. You can visit a museum there today.

EXPLORING CHEROKEE PLACES

Visitors can learn about the Cherokee at the New Echota State Historic Site in Calhoun, Georgia. The Cherokee Nation built its capital city there in 1825. The site shows how Cherokee people lived and worked just a few years before the Trail of Tears.

You can tour old Cherokee homes, shops, and barns. You can see the building where the first **Indigenous** American newspaper, the *Cherokee Phoenix*, was printed. You can visit a council house and courthouse that were important to the Cherokee government.

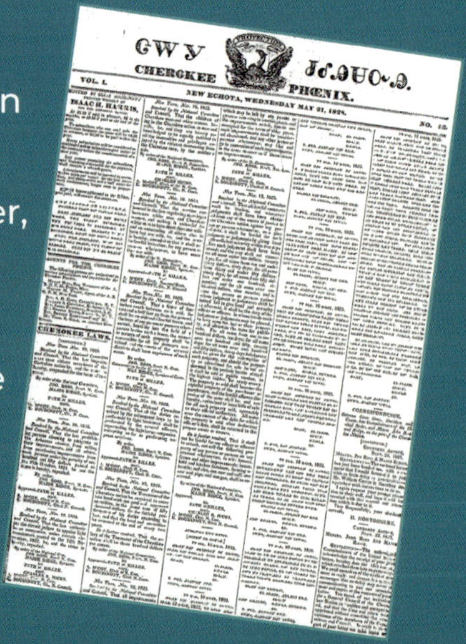
CHEROKEE PHŒNIX.
VOL. I.
NEW ECHOTA, WEDNESDAY MAY 21, 1828.

Culture Close-Up

In ancient times, the Cherokee built wattle and daub homes from sticks and mud. By the time New Echota was established, Cherokee people lived in log cabins just like other people in the region.

At the council, Cherokee Chief John Ross brought together tribes that had been forced to move to "Indian Country." The land later became Oklahoma and Kansas.

In Tahlequah, Oklahoma, you can visit the Cherokee National Peace Pavilion. The beautiful log structure was built to honor the place where the International Indian Council was held in 1843. The peaceful gathering brought together more than 18 Indigenous American tribes.

On the campus of Northeastern State University, you can visit Seminary Hall. The building was once part of the Cherokee Female Seminary. It was one of the first schools for girls west of the Mississippi River.

Culture Close-Up

The Cherokee Nation owns and operates 10 casinos in northeast Oklahoma. One is the Hard Rock Hotel & Casino in Tulsa.

THE CHEROKEE LANGUAGE

Tsalagi is the language of the Cherokee. People have spoken it for thousands of years. Thanks to a Cherokee man named Sequoyah, it was first written down about 200 years ago. He invented a system, called a **syllabary**, to match 85 symbols to the syllables of the spoken language.

Tsalagi is difficult to learn. Today, only about 2,000 people speak it well. The Cherokee Nation wants to change that. They helped create Tsalagi lessons that you can download on the free app Memrise.

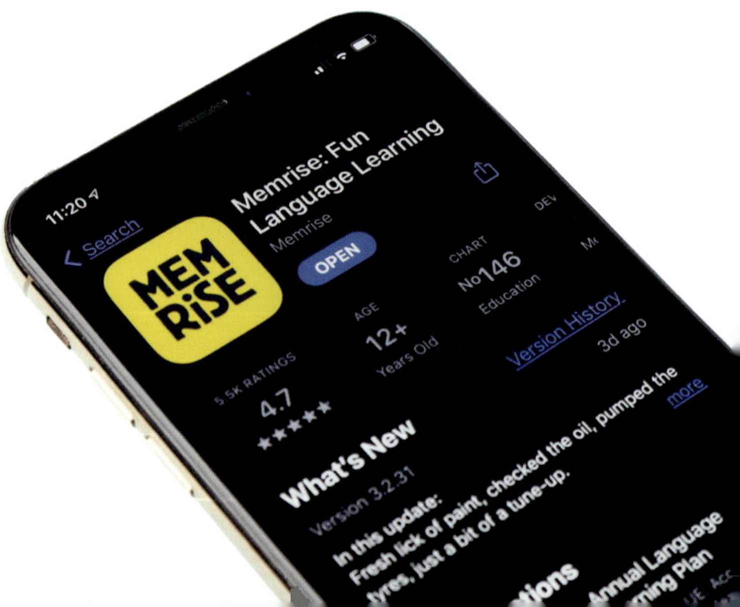

Using his system, Sequoyah quickly taught his daughter and other young Cherokees to read and write in Tsalagi.

Culture Close-Up

Practice these Cherokee phrases.

Osiyo. (Hello.)

Dtohitsu? (How are you?)

Gado detsadoa? (What is your name?)

Hatlv hinela? (Where do you live?)

Wado. (Thank you.)

HONORING CHEROKEE TRADITIONS

The Cherokee people have always told stories through music. Some songs make a connection to the spirit world. Some ask for healing or a good harvest. Traditionally, music was played with flutes, drums, and rattles. Today's artists add fiddles, guitars, and mandolins. Cherokee songs have strong beats that make them great for dancing!

Hip-hop artist Gary "Litefoot" Davis is a member of the Cherokee Nation. His rap music explores the history of the Cherokee people and their connection to the land.

Culture Close-Up

Litefoot is also a filmmaker and actor. He has appeared in *The Indian in the Cupboard* and the animated Netflix series *Spirit Rangers*.

Traditionally, Cherokee people grew squash, corn, and beans. They called these crops the "Three Sisters." When they were planted together, each helped the others grow. Cherokees also gathered ramps. These wild onions grow in the Appalachian Mountains.

Indigenous people from all over the Americas make dishes like Cherokee bean bread. Tamales are one version.

Cherokee people still enjoy these foods. One popular dish is bean bread. To make it, beans and corn are mashed to make a dough. The dough is shaped into patties, wrapped in corn leaves, and boiled.

In the spring, people still collect ramps. Some families have their own secret patches in the mountains.

Ancient Cherokee artists used natural materials like clay, wood, and bark. They made pottery. They created beautiful woven baskets. They used natural dyes to add bright colors.

Today, potter Jane Osti honors her Cherokee roots. She digs clay from native lands. She builds pots from coils of clay. She fires her creations in a pit dug outside, just like her ancestors did long ago.

Jane Osti

Martha Berry

Long ago, Cherokees traded with Europeans for glass beads. They used them to create beautiful designs. Today, Cherokee artist Martha Berry beads moccasins, belts, and sashes. Some have the Cherokee Sun Circle, a sacred symbol that represents living in balance with nature.

Culture Close-Up

Cherokee people still weave baskets by hand. They use river cane and other plants that grow in the Appalachian Mountains.

CHEROKEE CELEBRATIONS

The Cherokee National Holiday is celebrated each fall. It honors the signing of the Cherokee Nation Constitution in 1839. More than 150,000 people come to Oklahoma from around the world.

People listen to music and enjoy delicious foods. They play traditional Cherokee games such as hatchet throwing and marbles. The Principal Chief of the Cherokee Nation makes a speech.

The festival includes a **powwow** with dancers from many Indigenous American tribes. It lasts late into the night. Dancers compete for prizes.

A highlight of the Cherokee National Holiday is the parade. The newly crowned Miss Cherokee and Jr. Miss Cherokee ride on a decorated float. They serve as **ambassadors** for the Cherokee Nation. They teach others about Cherokee history, language, and culture.

Stickball teams also march in the parade. They show how to play the traditional Cherokee sport. Cherokee stickball is called *usdi danawa*, which means “little war.” Long ago, it was used to settle arguments between groups.

FAMOUS FACES

There are many famous Cherokees. Actor Wes Studi is a member of the Cherokee Nation. He has appeared in *Avatar*, *Spirit Rangers*, and many other productions. In 2019, he won an Academy Award.

Culture Close-Up

Wilma Mankiller was the first woman elected to be Principal Chief of the Cherokee Nation. She spent her life fighting for the rights of Indigenous Americans.

Will Rogers was a famous cowboy and comedian from the early 20th century. His father was a Cherokee senator who helped write the Oklahoma Constitution. Will Rogers appears in the *Guinness Book of World Records* for his lassoing skills.

LESSONS FROM THE CHEROKEE

Cherokee people celebrate their past, honor their **heritage**, and work together for their future. They remember their people's long history of showing respect for nature. Learning about Cherokee traditions can help all Americans take better care of our land and our communities.

GLOSSARY

ambassadors (am-BAS-uh-durz): people appointed to represent a nation or culture

colonizers (KAH-luh-nye-zerz): people who come to a new place and try to take control of the land and people they find there

eons (EE-ahnz): very long periods of time

heritage (HER-i-tij): traditions and beliefs that people consider to be an important part of their history

Indigenous (in-DI-juh-nuhs): the earliest known inhabitants of a place

pottery (PAH-tur-ee): objects made of baked clay, such as bowls and vases

powwow (POU-wou): a gathering of Indigenous Americans that is organized for social or ceremonial reasons and that may include traditional singing, dancing, and drumming

reservation (rez-ur-VAY-shuhn): an area of land set aside by the government for ownership by an Indigenous American tribe

sacred (SAY-krid): holy, very important, and deserving of great respect

settlers (SET-luhrz): people who make their homes in a new place and who have historically invaded and oppressed Indigenous peoples who originally lived there

syllabary (SIL-uh-bar-ee): a set of written characters that each represent a spoken syllable

FACT CHECK

1. The Cherokee Nation reservation is in ______.

   A. Tennessee B. Oklahoma C. the Appalachian Mountains

2. What three crops did the ancient Cherokee plant together?

   A. corn, beans, and squash B. peas, tomatoes, and peppers
   C. berries, wheat, and carrots

3. The Trail of Tears was a ______.

   A. monument B. road to the sea C. forced journey

4. _____ is the language of the Cherokee.

   A. Tsalagi B. Sequoyah C. Powwow

Answers: 1. B, 2. A, 3. C, 4. A

FURTHER READING

Ortiz, Simon. *The People Shall Continue*. Lee & Low Books, 2017.

Rogers, Andrea. *When We Gather (Ostadahlisiha): A Cherokee Tribal Feast*. HarperCollins, 2024.

Wagnon, Brad. *The Cherokee Syllabary: An Illustrated Key to the Cherokee Language*. 7th Generation, 2024.

ON THE INTERNET

Cherokee Nation
www.cherokee.org
Explore the official site of the Cherokee Nation.

Eastern Band of Cherokee Indians
ebci.com
Explore the official site of the Eastern Band of Cherokee Indians.

Native American Hall of Fame
nativehalloffame.org
Find biographies of well-known Indigenous Americans from the 1860s to the present.

INDEX

Appalachian Mountains 6, 18, 21

baskets 6, 20, 21

Cherokee National Holiday 22–25

New Echota 10, 11

Oklahoma 8, 9, 12, 13, 22, 27

pottery 6, 20

Ross, John 8, 12

Sequoyah 14, 15

Trail of Tears 8, 10

Tsalagi 14, 15

ABOUT THE AUTHOR

Anne Accardi is an author from Kansas City, Missouri. She is thrilled to share facts about Indigenous Americans with young people. She loves history and finding ways to connect the past with the present and future. When she's not reading or writing, you can find Anne in a library, museum, or movie theater.